GREAT MINDS® WIT & WISDOM

Grade 2 Module 2
The American West

Student Edition

© Great Minds PBC

GREAT MINDS

Great Minds® is the creator of *Eureka Math*®,
Wit & Wisdom®, *Alexandria Plan*™, and *PhD Science*®.

Published by Great Minds PBC
greatminds.org

© 2023 Great Minds PBC. All rights reserved. No part of this work may be reproduced or used in any form or by any means—graphic, electronic, or mechanical, including photocopying or information storage and retrieval systems—without written permission from the copyright holder.

Printed in the USA

A-Print

2 3 4 5 6 7 8 9 10 CCR 27 26 25 24

979-8-88588-730-4

STUDENT EDITION

Handout 2A: Fluency Homework

Handout 2B: Word Line

Handout 3A: Response Cards with Icons

Handout 3B: Topic-Specific Words

Handout 3C: Academic Vocabulary Sort

Handout 4A: Focusing Question Task 1 Evidence Organizer

Handout 4B: Topic-Specific Vocabulary Sort

Handout 4C: Informative Writing Checklist

Handout 6A: Fluency Homework

Handout 6B: Irregular Plural Nouns

Handout 7A: Main Topics and Details

Handout 7B: Irregular Plural Nouns

Handout 8A: Points that Support

Handout 8B: Irregular Plural Nouns

Handout 9A: Focusing Question Task 2 Evidence Organizer

Handout 9B: Informative Writing Checklist

Handout 10A: Socratic Seminar Self-Reflection

Handout 11A: Fluency Homework

Handout 12A: Main Events and Key Details

Handout 12B: Clearly Explained Details

Handout 12C: Capitalization

Handout 14A: Frayer Model

Handout 15A: Informative Writing Checklist

Handout 16A: Reader's Theater Script

Handout 18A: Mixed-Up Paragraph

Handout 19A: Informative Writing Checklist

Handout 19B: Identification and Explanation of Adverbs

Handout 20A: Fluency Homework

Handout 20B: Grammar Safari

Handout 21A: Digital Tool Checklist

Handout 21B: Past-Tense Verb Sort

Handout 22A: Evidence Organizer

Handout 22B: Irregular Past-Tense Verbs

Handout 24A: Johnny Appleseed Comparisons

Handout 24B: Informative Writing Checklist

Handout 24C: Frayer Model

Handout 26A: Fluency Homework

Handout 26B: Collective Nouns Brainstorm

Handout 27A: Collective Nouns

Handout 28A: Word Line

Handout 28B: Revise for Topic-Specific Words

Handout 29A: Prefix *un–*

Handout 30A: Focusing Question Task 6 Evidence Organizer

Handout 32A: Informative Writing Checklist

Handout 33A: Evidence Organizer for End-of-Module Task Practice

Handout 34A: End-of-Module Evidence Organizer

Handout 35A: Informative Writing Checklist

Volume of Reading Reflection Questions

Wit & Wisdom Family Tip Sheet

Name:

Handout 2A: Fluency Homework

Directions: Read the text for homework. Have an adult or peer initial the unshaded boxes each day that you read the passage.

Buffalo Dusk

The buffaloes are gone.

And those who saw the buffaloes are gone.

Those who saw the buffaloes by thousands and how they pawed the prairie sod into dust

with their hoofs, their great heads down pawing on in a great pageant of dusk,

Those who saw the buffaloes are gone.

And the buffaloes are gone.

57 words

Sandburg, Carl. *Smoke and Steel*. New York: Harcourt, Brace, and Howe, 1920.

Student Performance Checklist:	Day 1		Day 2		Day 3		Day 4	
	You	Listener*	You	Listener*	You	Listener*	You	Listener*
Read the passage three to five times.								
Read with appropriate phrasing and pausing.								
Read with appropriate expression.								
Read at a good pace, not too fast and not too slow.								
Read to be heard and understood.								

*Adult or peer

G2 > M2 > Handout 2B · WIT & WISDOM®

Name:

Handout 2B: Word Line

Directions:

1. Cut out the words.

2. Arrange the words in order of their strength on the word line below to the right and left of walked.

walked

gallop__ed__

roam__ed__

rush__ed__

wobbl__ed__

charg__ed__

Name:

Handout 3A: Response Cards with Icons

Directions: Cut on the dotted lines.

Buffalo

American Indians

Government

Prairie: The Grasses

Settlers

President Theodore Roosevelt

Name:

Handout 3B: Topic-Specific Words

Directions: Read the sentences. Circle words that are <u>not</u> topic-specific. Near each circled word, write a topic-specific word to replace the circled word.

1. (People) wanted to hurt (others), so they killed (animals).
   settlers — indians — buffalo

2. Workers taught some (people) how to make the (land) healthy again.
   farmers — grass

3. The buffalo's (legs) poked holes in the ground, which helped plants get (water).
   hooves — moisture

Name:

Handout 3C: Academic Vocabulary Sort

Directions:

1. Cut out the words at the bottom of the page.

2. Sort the words into the correct category.

Like *tough*	**Unlike** *tough*

| withered | crumbled | healthy |
| fragile | survived | strong |

Name:

Handout 4A: Focusing Question Task 1 Evidence Organizer

Directions: Record evidence to include in your informative paragraph.

People's Impact on the Prairie		
First, American Indians …	Then, settlers …	Finally, the Roosevelt government …

Name:

Handout 4B:
Topic-Specific Vocabulary Sort

Directions:

1. Cut the word cards apart.
2. Sort the words into categories.
3. Discuss your thinking with your partner.

   "I think _____ and _____ belong together in a category called _____ because _____."

buffalo	withered	protected	bison
crumbled	graze	prairie	herd
extinct	roam	grass	settlers
American Indians	battle	explorers	government
hunters	drought	plains	hooves

Name:

Handout 4C: Informative Writing Checklist

Directions: After completing your informative paragraph, circle 🙂 Yes or 😐 Not Yet to answer each prompt. Be sure to include a writing goal.

Reading Comprehension	Self	Peer	Teacher
I understand the impact of the American Indians, settlers, and the Roosevelt government on the prairie.	Yes Not Yet	Yes Not Yet	Yes Not Yet
Structure	Self	Peer	Teacher
I include a topic statement.	Yes Not Yet	Yes Not Yet	Yes Not Yet
I include at least three evidence sentences.	Yes Not Yet	Yes Not Yet	Yes Not Yet
I use temporal words like *first*, *then*, and *finally* in the correct order.	Yes Not Yet	Yes Not Yet	Yes Not Yet

	Self	Peer	Teacher
I end the paragraph with a conclusion.	😊 😐 Yes Not Yet	😊 😐 Yes Not Yet	😊 😐 Yes Not Yet
Development	Self	Peer	Teacher
My evidence relates to the topic and helps develop my points.	😊 😐 Yes Not Yet	😊 😐 Yes Not Yet	😊 😐 Yes Not Yet
Style	Self	Peer	Teacher
I use topic-specific words.	😊 😐 Yes Not Yet	😊 😐 Yes Not Yet	😊 😐 Yes Not Yet
Conventions	Self	Peer	Teacher
I use capital letters at the beginning of sentences and proper nouns. **ABC**	😊 😐 Yes Not Yet	😊 😐 Yes Not Yet	😊 😐 Yes Not Yet
I use end punctuation. **. ? !**	😊 😐 Yes Not Yet	😊 😐 Yes Not Yet	😊 😐 Yes Not Yet

Name:

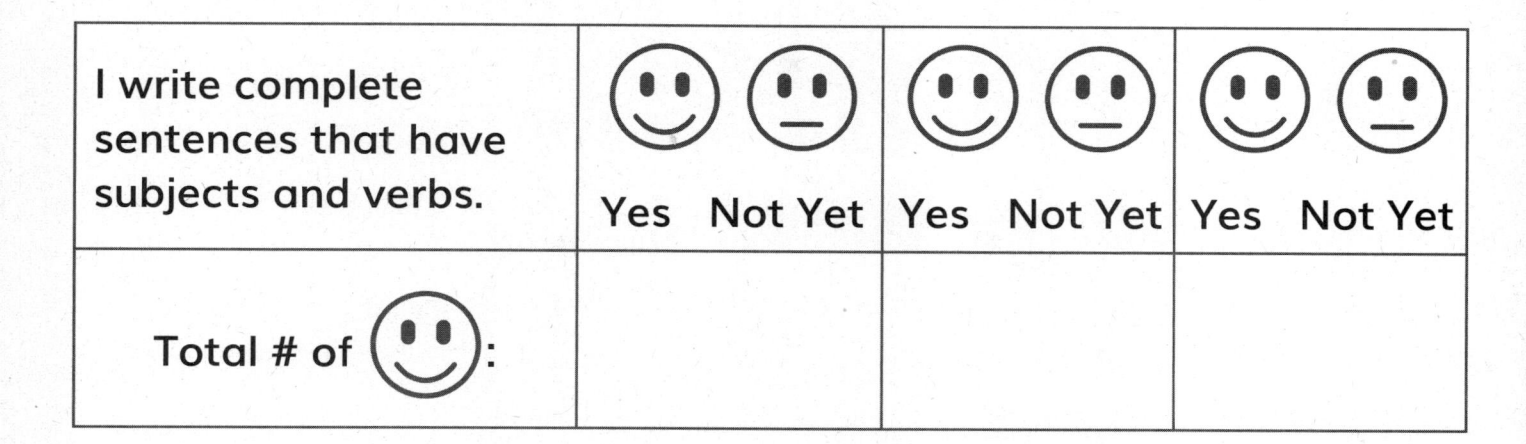

I write complete sentences that have subjects and verbs.	☺ ☹ Yes Not Yet	☺ ☹ Yes Not Yet	☺ ☹ Yes Not Yet
Total # of ☺ :			

My writing goal is _____

_____

_____

Teacher Feedback

Name:

Handout 6A: Fluency Homework

Directions: Choose one of the text options to read for homework. Have an adult or peer initial the unshaded boxes each day that you read the passage.

Option A

> By taking care of the grass, the Indians took care of the buffalo. In return, the buffalo took care of the Indians and the plains. Buffalo were the Indians' food. They were used to make their shelter and clothing.
>
> 39 words
>
> Jean Craighead George, *The Buffalo Are Back*. New York: Dutton Children's Books, 2010.

G2 > M2 > Handout 6A • WIT & WISDOM®

Student Performance Checklist:	Day 1 You	Day 1 Listener*	Day 2 You	Day 2 Listener	Day 3 You	Day 3 Listener*	Day 4 You	Day 4 Listener*
Accurately read the passage three to five times.								
Read with appropriate phrasing and pausing.	▓							
Read with appropriate expression.	▓		▓					
Read at a good pace, not too fast and not too slow.	▓		▓	▓	▓	▓		
Read to be heard and understood.	▓		▓	▓	▓	▓		

*Adult or peer

Name:

Option B

> But there was trouble on the plains. The government broke its treaties with the Indians. So the Indians fought back and won several battles against the United States Army. Then the government saw another way to defeat the Indians. Soldiers and settlers were encouraged to shoot every buffalo they saw, or drive whole herds over cliffs. Without the buffalo for food, shelter, and clothing, the Indians could not survive on the plains.
>
> 72 words
>
> Jean Craighead George, *The Buffalo Are Back*. New York: Dutton Children's Books, 2010.

Student Performance Checklist:	Day 1 You	Day 1 Listener*	Day 2 You	Day 2 Listener	Day 3 You	Day 3 Listener*	Day 4 You	Day 4 Listener*
Read the passage three to five times.								
Read with appropriate phrasing and pausing.	▓	▓						
Read with appropriate expression.	▓	▓	▓	▓				
Read at a good pace, not too fast and not too slow.	▓	▓	▓	▓	▓	▓		
Read to be heard and understood.	▓	▓	▓	▓	▓	▓		

*Adult or peer

Name:

Handout 6B: Irregular Plural Nouns

Directions: Cut the cards apart and sort by whether the words are regular or irregular plural nouns.

REGULAR ADDS "S" OR "ES" TO MAKE THE NOUN PLURAL	IRREGULAR DOESN'T JUST ADD "S" OR "ES"
HORSE to HORSES	TOOTH to TEETH
WOMAN to WOMEN	CHILD to CHILDREN
MAN to MEN	FOOT to FEET
TRIBE to TRIBES	MEAT to MEAT
PERSON to PEOPLE	INDIAN to INDIANS
SETTLER to SETTLERS	BISON to BISON

Name:

Handout 7A: Main Topics and Details

Directions: Cut on dotted lines. Place buttons and bag pictures on the left column of the chart and record details and main topics in the right column.

Name:

Pages:	Main Topic and Details

Name: _____

Handout 7B: Irregular Plural Nouns

Directions:

1. Read the sentences below.
2. Ask yourself, "Is this a word I can add –s or –es to, or is it an irregular one?"
3. Think about where you have seen the word before or a time you have used it while speaking.
4. Circle the correct form of the plural noun. Write it on the line. Read it aloud one more time.

1. A herd of _____ charged across a grassy
   (bisons, bison)

   plain, their hooves rumbling.

2. In some tribes, membership was passed on from mothers to their

   _____ .
   (childs, children, childrens)

3. There are many different _____ , or groups of
   (tribe, tribes)

   American Indians who share a culture.

4. Indian _____ hunted and decided whether to
   (mans, mens, men)

   go to war.

Name:

Handout 8A: Points That Support

Directions: Sort the points into evidence that supports the topic statement, and evidence that does not.

Topic Statement:
  Farming provided food and wealth from eastern Plains Indians.

Possible Points

Plains Indians ate a lot of corn.

Beans climbed up corn stalks like a pole.

Village tribes got most of their food from farming.

The fertile land helped food grow.

Plains Indians made farming tools from animals.

Tribes grew extra food and traded it for new things.

Name:

Handout 8B: Irregular Plural Nouns

Directions: Work with a partner to write captions for the photos listed. Include an irregular plural noun in each sentence. Underline the irregular plural noun. After writing the captions, write the plural nouns you used in their singular and plural forms in the chart that follows.

Page	Caption
14	
19	
21	
27	

Singular	Plural

Name:

Handout 9A: Focusing Question Task 2 Evidence Organizer

Directions: Find evidence about each topic. Write words or phrases in the boxes about important points that develop the topic statement.

Topic Statement:
Draft 1: The Plains Indians used plants to help them survive.
Draft 2: The Plains Indians used animals to help them survive.

Point	Plants	Animals
1		
2		
3		
4		

Name:

Handout 9B:
Informative Writing Checklist

Directions: After completing your informative paragraph, circle 😊 Yes or 😐 Not Yet to answer each prompt. Be sure to include a writing goal.

Reading Comprehension	Self	Peer	Teacher
I understand how the Plains Indians used plants or animals.	Yes Not Yet	Yes Not Yet	Yes Not Yet
Structure	**Self**	**Peer**	**Teacher**
I include a topic statement.	Yes Not Yet	Yes Not Yet	Yes Not Yet
I include at least two points with evidence.	Yes Not Yet	Yes Not Yet	Yes Not Yet
I end the paragraph with a conclusion.	Yes Not Yet	Yes Not Yet	Yes Not Yet

Development	Self	Peer	Teacher
I choose important points that support the topic statement.	☺ ☺ Yes Not Yet	☺ ☺ Yes Not Yet	☺ ☺ Yes Not Yet

Style	Self	Peer	Teacher
I use topic-specific words.	☺ ☺ Yes Not Yet	☺ ☺ Yes Not Yet	☺ ☺ Yes Not Yet
I use simple and compound sentences.	☺ ☺ Yes Not Yet	☺ ☺ Yes Not Yet	☺ ☺ Yes Not Yet
I combine sentences using *and*, *but*, and *so*.	☺ ☺ Yes Not Yet	☺ ☺ Yes Not Yet	☺ ☺ Yes Not Yet

Conventions	Self	Peer	Teacher
I use capital letters at the beginning of sentences and proper nouns. **A B C**	☺ ☺ Yes Not Yet	☺ ☺ Yes Not Yet	☺ ☺ Yes Not Yet
I use end punctuation. **. ? !**	☺ ☺ Yes Not Yet	☺ ☺ Yes Not Yet	☺ ☺ Yes Not Yet
I write complete sentences that have subjects and verbs.	☺ ☺ Yes Not Yet	☺ ☺ Yes Not Yet	☺ ☺ Yes Not Yet
Total # of ☺:			

Name:

My writing goal is _____

_____

_____

_____

_____

_____

Teacher Feedback

Name: _____

Handout 10A:
Socratic Seminar Self-Reflection

Directions: Use one of the letters below to describe how often you performed each action during the Socratic Seminar.

A = I always did that.

S = I sometimes did that.

N = I'll do that next time.

Expectation	Evaluation (A, S, N)
I noticed the whole message.	
I linked what I said to what others said.	
I looked at the speaker.	
I spoke only when no one else was speaking.	
I used kind words.	
I varied inflection when speaking.	

Name:

Handout 11A: Fluency Homework

Directions: Choose one of the text options to read for homework. Have an adult or peer initial the unshaded boxes each day that you read the passage.

Option A

> Today, we said our last goodbyes. Grandma hugged me so tight I almost stopped breathing. Ma cried when friends gave her a friendship quilt. Pa had tears in his eyes, too. I wondered why everyone was so sad. Ma told me later that we might not see many of these people ever again. I didn't want to believe her, but Ma never lies.
>
> 63 words
>
> Murphy, Patricia J. *Journey of a Pioneer*. New York: Dorling Kindersley Limited, 2008.

Student Performance Checklist:	Day 1		Day 2		Day 3		Day 4	
	You	Listener*	You	Listener	You	Listener*	You	Listener*
Read the passage three to five times.								
Read with appropriate phrasing and pausing.	▓	▓						
Read with appropriate expression.	▓	▓	▓	▓				
Read at a good pace, not too fast and not too slow.	▓	▓	▓	▓	▓	▓		
Read to be heard and understood.	▓	▓	▓	▓	▓	▓		

*Adult or peer

Name:

Option B

After endless prairies, we've finally reached mountains, but climbing the **steep** sides is hard work! To go up, we have to lighten our load, which means dumping Ma's stove and trunk. To get down, we tie rope to a tree and then the back of the wagon. Then we slowly let out the rope. The Rocky Mountains are too steep. Luckily, we used a flat, wide path through them called the South Pass. Oregon Territory is close!

77 words

Murphy, Patricia J. *Journey of a Pioneer*. New York: Dorling Kindersley Limited, 2008.

Student Performance Checklist:	Day 1 You	Day 1 Listener*	Day 2 You	Day 2 Listener	Day 3 You	Day 3 Listener*	Day 4 You	Day 4 Listener*
Read the passage three to five times.								
Read with appropriate phrasing and pausing.								
Read with appropriate expression.								
Read at a good pace, not too fast and not too slow.								
Read to be heard and understood.								

*Adult or peer

Name:

Handout 12A:
Main Events and Key Details

Directions: Cut on the dotted lines. Match the key details to the main events.

MAIN EVENTS

Olivia and her family prepare and head out on the Oregon Trail (March–April 1845).

Olivia and her family face challenges on the trail.

Olivia and her family arrive in Oregon Territory (September 1845).

Name:

KEY DETAILS

Olivia and her family cross a river.

Olivia and her family say goodbye to their friends.

Olivia and her family reach the "jumping off point."

Olivia and her family celebrate!

Olivia and her family reach the mountains.

Olivia has to say goodbye to her friend Lizzie.

Pa tells Olivia they are moving west.

Olivia and her family pick a plot of land for their home.

Name:

Handout 12B: Clearly Explained Details

Directions: Follow along as the teacher reads aloud. Then, highlight the topic statement and underline each important detail.

Passage 1:

1. The fire was good for the prairie. 2. The calf may have been afraid of the flames, but they kept the trees from taking over the grasslands. 3. The fire's ashes put nutrients into the soil making the grass healthier for the buffalo that ate it.

Passage 2 (Extension Activity):

1. As the dust storms attacked farms and cities, the government worked to save the prairie. 2. Farmers were taught to plant and grow crops in curves, instead of straight lines. 3. The contour plowing helped to prevent dirt from blowing away. 4. Government workers planted trees with deep roots to hold moisture in the soil and break the wind. 5. When the rains returned, farmers planted grass between their curving rows of corn to hold the soil in place. 6. Crops flourished again.

Name:

Handout 12C: Capitalization

Directions: Correct the capitalization mistake in each sentence. Then, explain why it is a mistake.

Writers capitalize:

- The word "I"

- The beginning of a sentence.

- Dates

- Names of people, places, and holidays.

Correct the mistake	Explain the mistake
Ma said oregon territory is far away and it will take many months to get there.	Oregon Territory
Pioneers try to get to Wyoming before the fourth of july.	Fourth of July
We arrive at our Home in Oregon.	home
Pioneers traveled along the oregon trail	Oregon Trail
Climbing up the steep Mountain is hard work.	mautain

Name:

Handout 14A: Frayer Model

Directions: Complete the Frayer Model for *tragedy*.

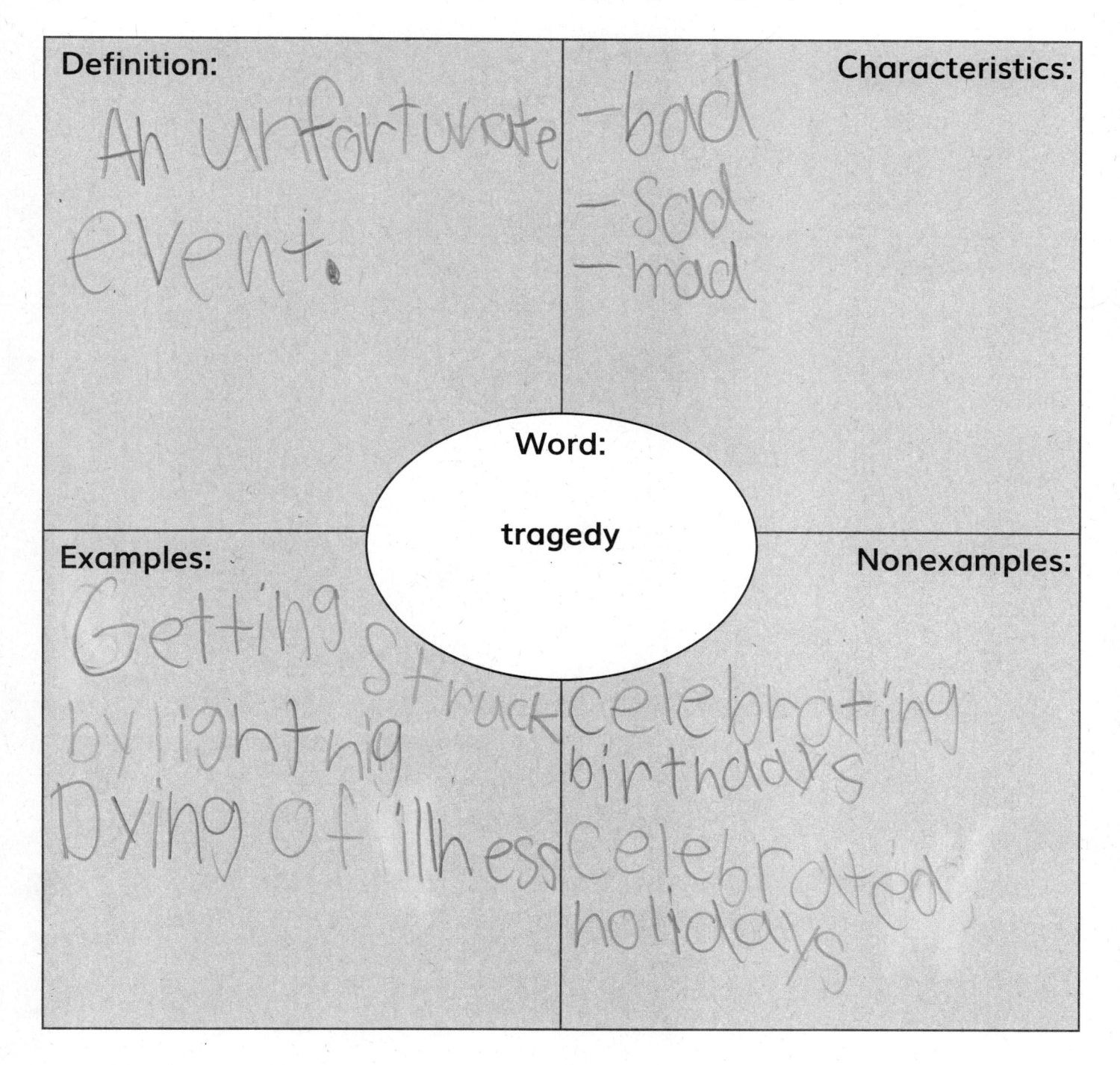

Definition:	Characteristics:
An unfortunate event.	– bad – sad – mad

Word: tragedy

Examples:	Nonexamples:
Getting struck by lightnig Dying of illness	celebrating birthdays celebrated holidays

Name: _____

Handout 15A:
Informative Writing Checklist

Directions: After completing your informative paragraph, circle 🙂 Yes or 😐 Not Yet to answer each prompt. Be sure to include a writing goal.

Reading Comprehension	Self	Peer	Teacher
I understand how the pioneers responded to challenges.	🙂 Yes 😐 Not Yet	🙂 Yes 😐 Not Yet	🙂 Yes 😐 Not Yet
Structure	**Self**	**Peer**	**Teacher**
I include a topic statement.	🙂 Yes 😐 Not Yet	🙂 Yes 😐 Not Yet	🙂 Yes 😐 Not Yet
I include at least two points with evidence.	🙂 Yes 😐 Not Yet	🙂 Yes 😐 Not Yet	🙂 Yes 😐 Not Yet
I end the paragraph with a conclusion.	🙂 Yes 😐 Not Yet	🙂 Yes 😐 Not Yet	🙂 Yes 😐 Not Yet
Development	**Self**	**Peer**	**Teacher**
I choose important points that support the topic statement.	🙂 Yes 😐 Not Yet	🙂 Yes 😐 Not Yet	🙂 Yes 😐 Not Yet

	Self	Peer	Teacher
I clearly explain my points using details.	😊 😐 Yes Not Yet	😊 😐 Yes Not Yet	😊 😐 Yes Not Yet
Style	Self	Peer	Teacher
I use topic-specific words.	😊 😐 Yes Not Yet	😊 😐 Yes Not Yet	😊 😐 Yes Not Yet
Conventions	Self	Peer	Teacher
I use capital letters at the beginning of sentences and proper nouns. **ABC**	😊 😐 Yes Not Yet	😊 😐 Yes Not Yet	😊 😐 Yes Not Yet
I use end punctuation. **. ? !**	😊 😐 Yes Not Yet	😊 😐 Yes Not Yet	😊 😐 Yes Not Yet
I write complete sentences that have subjects and verbs.	😊 😐 Yes Not Yet	😊 😐 Yes Not Yet	😊 😐 Yes Not Yet
Total # of 😊:			

Name:

My writing goal is _____

_____

_____

Teacher Feedback

Name:

Handout 16A: Reader's Theater Script

Adapted from excerpts of *The Legend of the Bluebonnet* **by Tomie dePaola**

Directions: Read through the script. Highlight your part wherever it appears on the script. Practice as fluency homework and with your small group. Remember to vary your inflection.

Characters:

- Dancers
- She-Who-Is-Alone
- Narrator

Section 1: Adapted from pages 3–9

Dancers:	Our land is dying. Our People are dying, too. We do not know what we have done to anger the Great Spirits. Great Spirits, tell us what we must do so you will send the rain that will bring back life.
Narrator:	For three days, the dancers danced to the sound of the drums. For three days, the People called Comanche watched and waited. And even though the hard winter was over, no healing rains came.
	Among the few children left was a small girl named She-Who-Is-Alone. She sat by herself watching the dancers.

She-Who-Is-Alone: Here is my doll made from buckskin—a warrior doll. I painted the eyes, nose, and mouth on with the juice of berries. Here on its head are brilliant blue feathers from the bird who cries "Jay-jay-jay." My mother made the doll, and my father bought the blue feathers. I love the doll very much.

Section 2: Adapted from pages 27–29

Narrator: And as the People sang and danced their thanks to the Great Spirits, a warm rain began to fall and the land began to live again.

Dancers: [Speaking to She-Who-Is-Alone] We named you "She-Who-Is-Alone," but now you will be known by another name—"One-Who-Dearly-Loved-Her-People."

Narrator: And every spring, the Great Spirits remember the sacrifice of a little girl. They fill the hills and valleys of the land, now called Texas, with the beautiful blue flowers.

Name:

Handout 19A: Informative Writing Checklist

Directions: After completing your informative paragraph, circle ☺ Yes or ☹ Not Yet to answer each prompt. Be sure to include a writing goal.

Reading Comprehension	Self	Peer	Teacher
I understand the life lesson of *Bluebonnet*.	☺ Yes ☹ Not Yet	☺ Yes ☹ Not Yet	☺ Yes ☹ Not Yet
Structure	**Self**	**Peer**	**Teacher**
I start the paragraph with an introduction.	☺ Yes ☹ Not Yet	☺ Yes ☹ Not Yet	☺ Yes ☹ Not Yet
I include a topic statement.	☺ Yes ☹ Not Yet	☺ Yes ☹ Not Yet	☺ Yes ☹ Not Yet
I include at least two points with evidence.	☺ Yes ☹ Not Yet	☺ Yes ☹ Not Yet	☺ Yes ☹ Not Yet
I end the paragraph with a conclusion.	☺ Yes ☹ Not Yet	☺ Yes ☹ Not Yet	☺ Yes ☹ Not Yet

Development	Self	Peer	Teacher
I choose important points that support the topic statement.	☺ ☺ Yes Not Yet	☺ ☺ Yes Not Yet	☺ ☺ Yes Not Yet
I clearly explain my points using details.	☺ ☺ Yes Not Yet	☺ ☺ Yes Not Yet	☺ ☺ Yes Not Yet
Style	**Self**	**Peer**	**Teacher**
I use topic-specific words.	☺ ☺ Yes Not Yet	☺ ☺ Yes Not Yet	☺ ☺ Yes Not Yet
Conventions	**Self**	**Peer**	**Teacher**
I use end punctuation. . ? !	☺ ☺ Yes Not Yet	☺ ☺ Yes Not Yet	☺ ☺ Yes Not Yet
I write complete sentences that have subjects and verbs.	☺ ☺ Yes Not Yet	☺ ☺ Yes Not Yet	☺ ☺ Yes Not Yet
Total # of ☺ :			

Name:

My writing goal is _____

_____

_____

Teacher Feedback

Name:

Handout 19B: Identification and Explanation of Adverbs

Directions:

1. Read the sentence.
   Underline the verb.
2. Circle the adverb (word with –ly).
3. Explain the adverb.

Example:

"She took it and (quietly) crept out into the night."

Explain: She _____crept_____ in a _____quiet_____ way.
　　　　　　　　(action)

"She held her doll tightly to her heart."
Explain: She _____ the doll in a _____ way.
　　　　　　　　(action)

"Horses let Plains Indians travel quickly."
Explain: Plains Indians _____ in a _____ way.
　　　　　　　　　　　　(action)

"The lark sang sweetly."
Explain: The bird _____ in a _____ way.
　　　　　　　　　(action)

"The Plains Indians proudly keep alive their traditions."
Explain:
The Plains Indians _____ alive their traditions in a _____ way.
　　　　　　　　　(action)

Write your own sentence:

Tightly: _____

Quickly: _____

Sweetly: _____

Quietly: _____

Name:

Handout 20A: Fluency Homework

Directions: Choose one of the text options to read for homework. Have an adult or peer initial the unshaded boxes each day that you read the passage.

Option A

> As he walked, John planted seeds. He gave a small bagful to everyone he saw. Soon, everyone who knew him called him Johnny Appleseed.
>
> Sometimes Johnny stopped for many weeks, helping the pioneers. They cleared the land. They built homes. They planted rows and rows of apple trees. When they were finished, Johnny walked on to help others. But he always came back to see his friends.
>
> 67 words
>
> Aliki, *The Story of Johnny Appleseed.* New York: Aladdin Paperbacks, 1963

Student Performance Checklist:	Day 1 You	Day 1 Listener*	Day 2 You	Day 2 Listener	Day 3 You	Day 3 Listener*	Day 4 You	Day 4 Listener*
Read the passage three to five times.								
Read with appropriate phrasing and pausing.								
Read with appropriate expression.								
Read at a good pace, not too fast and not too slow.								
Read to be heard and understood.								

*Adult or peer

Name:

Option B

Johnny met many Indians on the way. He was kind to them and gave them seeds and herbs, which they used as medicine. Although the Indians were not friendly to any white men who chased them from their homes, Johnny was their friend.

Johnny did not like people to fight. He tried to make peace between the settlers and the Indians, for he believed that all men should live together as brothers.

72 words

Aliki, *The Story of Johnny Appleseed*. New York: Aladdin Paperbacks, 1963.

Student Performance Checklist:	Day 1		Day 2		Day 3		Day 4	
	You	Listener*	You	Listener	You	Listener*	You	Listener*
Read the passage three to five times.								
Read with appropriate phrasing and pausing.								
Read with appropriate expression.								
Read at a good pace, not too fast and not too slow.								
Read to be heard and understood.								

*Adult or peer

Name:

Handout 20B: Grammar Safari

Directions: Go on a Grammar Safari for verbs. Then, sort the verbs as past or present tense.

Jot down the verbs you find as you read the assigned pages.

Sort your verbs as past tense or present tense.

Past Tense	Present Tense

Name:

Handout 21A: Digital Tool Checklist

Directions: Complete this checklist by experimenting with bookmaking features. Try every feature and check each off the list.

Features	Checkmarks
I created a new book.	
I changed the background color or pattern.	
I added text by typing my name.	
I selected my name.	
I changed the *size* of my name.	
I changed the *font* of my name.	
I changed the *color* of my name.	
I changed my text using bold, *italic,* or underline.	
I moved my name around the page.	
I used the drawing feature to add a picture of an apple.	
I used undo and delete.	
I added a photo.	
I recorded myself saying my name and listened to it.	
I added another page.	
I saved my book.	

Name:

Handout 21B: Past-Tense Verb Sort

Directions:

1. Cut apart the word cards below.
2. Say each word in a sentence to your partner.
3. Sort the words into two categories: regular verbs and irregular verbs.

sat	felt	looked	gathered
roamed	built	flew	took
ate	sold	called	thought
came	helped	bought	saw
rested	gave	REGULAR VERBS	IRREGULAR VERBS

Name:

Handout 22A:
Evidence Organizer Chart

Directions: Record evidence for the lesson of *The Story of Johnny Appleseed*. Write the lesson of the story.

Pages	Evidence

The lesson of *The Story of Johnny Appleseed* is ...

Name:

Handout 22B:
Irregular Past-Tense Verbs

Directions:

1. Read the sentence.

2. Change the underlined word to its past-tense form.

3. Write a new sentence in the past tense.

In their covered wagons, the pioneers **make** a long and dangerous journey.

Past-Tense Form: _____

_____

Everyone **knows** Johnny Appleseed.

Past-Tense Form: _____

_____

The pioneers **build** homes.

Past-Tense Form: _____

_____

Johnny always **comes** back to see his friends.

Past-Tense Form: _____

_____

INDEPENDENT WORK

The mother bear **comes** and **sees** them playing together.

Past-Tense Form: _____

_____

He **meets** wolves and foxes.

Past-Tense Form: _____

_____

Name:

Handout 24A:
Johnny Appleseed Comparisons

Directions: Use the Aliki and Kellogg texts to find examples of text details and illustration details about the major event "Johnny becomes ill."

Major Event: Johnny becomes ill.		
	Aliki	Kellogg
Details in text		
Details in illustrations		

Name:

Handout 24B:
Informative Writing Checklist

Directions: After completing your informative paragraph, circle ☺ Yes or ☹ Not Yet to answer each prompt. Be sure to include a writing goal.

Reading Comprehension	Self	Peer	Teacher
I understand the lesson of the story of Johnny Appleseed.	☺ Yes ☹ Not Yet	☺ Yes ☹ Not Yet	☺ Yes ☹ Not Yet
Structure	**Self**	**Peer**	**Teacher**
I start the paragraph with an introduction.	☺ Yes ☹ Not Yet	☺ Yes ☹ Not Yet	☺ Yes ☹ Not Yet
I include a topic statement.	☺ Yes ☹ Not Yet	☺ Yes ☹ Not Yet	☺ Yes ☹ Not Yet
I include at least two points with evidence.	☺ Yes ☹ Not Yet	☺ Yes ☹ Not Yet	☺ Yes ☹ Not Yet
I end the paragraph with a conclusion.	☺ Yes ☹ Not Yet	☺ Yes ☹ Not Yet	☺ Yes ☹ Not Yet

Development	Self	Peer	Teacher
I choose important points that support the topic statement.	😊 😐 Yes Not Yet	😊 😐 Yes Not Yet	😊 😐 Yes Not Yet
I clearly explain my points using details.	😊 😐 Yes Not Yet	😊 😐 Yes Not Yet	😊 😐 Yes Not Yet
Research Extension (optional): I include a fun fact about the real John Chapman.	😊 😐 Yes Not Yet	😊 😐 Yes Not Yet	😊 😐 Yes Not Yet
Style	**Self**	**Peer**	**Teacher**
I use topic-specific words.	😊 😐 Yes Not Yet	😊 😐 Yes Not Yet	😊 😐 Yes Not Yet
I use photos or drawings to support the writing.	😊 😐 Yes Not Yet	😊 😐 Yes Not Yet	😊 😐 Yes Not Yet
Digital Tools	**Self**	**Peer**	**Teacher**
My book includes photos and drawings that support my writing.	😊 😐 Yes Not Yet	😊 😐 Yes Not Yet	😊 😐 Yes Not Yet
I include at least one audio recording of me reading a page aloud.	😊 😐 Yes Not Yet	😊 😐 Yes Not Yet	😊 😐 Yes Not Yet
Total # of 😊:			

Name:

My writing goal is _____

_____

_____

Teacher Feedback

Name:

Handout 24C: Frayer Model

Directions: Complete the Frayer Model for *shelter*.

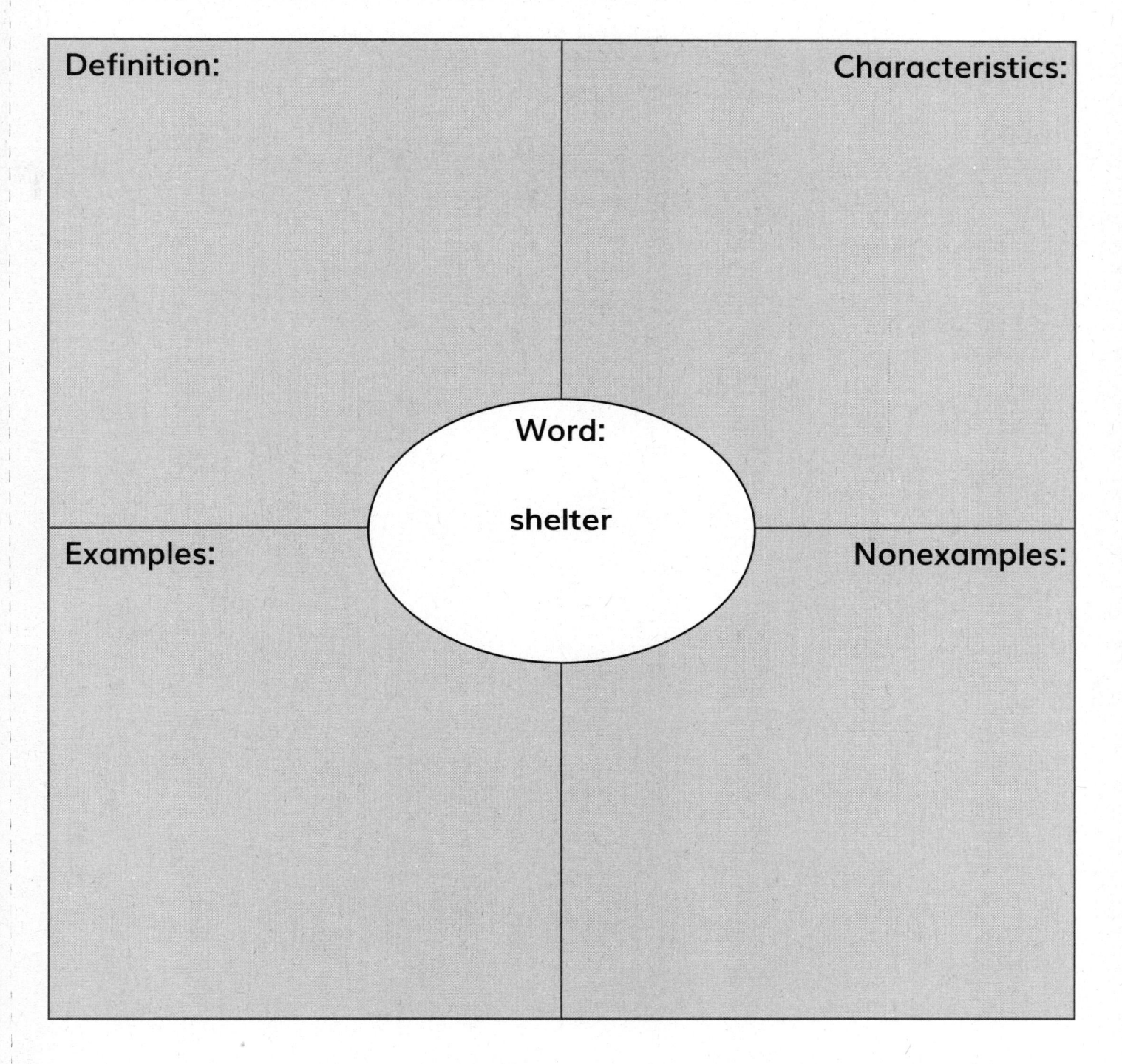

Definition:	Characteristics:
Examples:	Nonexamples:

Word:

shelter

Name:

Handout 26A: Fluency Homework

Directions: Choose one of the text options to read for homework. Have an adult or peer initial the unshaded boxes each day that you read the passage.

Option A

> Whoop! Clang! Whoop! Bang! John Henry's hammer whistled as he swung it. Chug, chug! Clatter! rattled the machine. Hour after hour raced by. The machine was ahead! "Hand me that twenty-pound hammer, L'il Bill!" Harder and faster crashed the hammer. Great chunks of rock fell as John Henry ripped hole after hole into the tunnel wall. The machine rattled and whistled and drilled even faster.
>
> 65 words
>
> **Keats, Ezra Jack.** *John Henry: An American Legend.* **New York: Dragonfly Books, 1965.**

Student Performance Checklist:	Day 1 You	Day 1 Listener*	Day 2 You	Day 2 Listener*	Day 3 You	Day 3 Listener*	Day 4 You	Day 4 Listener*
Read the passage three to five times.								
Read with appropriate phrasing and pausing.								
Read with appropriate expression.								
Read at a good pace, not too fast and not too slow.								
Read to be heard and understood.								

*Adult or peer

Name:

Option B

Suddenly there was a great crash. Light streamed into the dark tunnel. John Henry had broken through! Wild cries of joy burst from the men. Still holding one of his hammers, John Henry stepped out into the glowing light of a dying day. It was the last step he ever took. Even the great heart of John Henry could not bear the strain of his last task. John Henry died with his hammer in his hand.

76 words

Keats, Ezra Jack. *John Henry: An American Legend*. New York: Dragonfly Books, 1965.

G2 > M2 > Handout 26A • WIT & WISDOM®

Student Performance Checklist:	Day 1 You	Day 1 Listener*	Day 2 You	Day 2 Listener*	Day 3 You	Day 3 Listener*	Day 4 You	Day 4 Listener*	Day 5 You	Day 5 Listener*
Read the passage three to five times.										
Read with appropriate phrasing and pausing.	▓	▓								
Read with appropriate expression.	▓	▓	▓	▓						
Read at a good pace, not too fast and not too slow.	▓	▓	▓	▓	▓	▓				
Read to be heard and understood.	▓	▓	▓	▓	▓	▓				

*Adult or peer

Name: _____

Handout 26B:
Collective Nouns Brainstorm

Directions:

1. Think of collective nouns in the module books or in the world around you.
2. Write the collective noun.
3. Draw a sketch of the group it describes and write the name of the objects in the group.

Collective Noun	Sketch	Names a group of ...
Example: herd		buffalo/bison

Collective Noun	Sketch	Names a group of ...

Name: _____

Handout 27A: Collective Nouns

Directions: Write a sentence and draw a picture to go with the collective nouns listed.

Collective noun: herd

Sentence: _____

_____

Sketch:

Collective noun: orchard

Sentence: _____

_____

Sketch:

Collective noun: tribe

Sentence: _____

_____

Sketch:

Name: _____

Handout 28A: Word Line

Directions:

1. Cut apart the word cards.
2. Arrange the words on the word line in order of their strength from quietest to loudest.

silent	groaned	shouted
shrieked	roared	soundlessly
whisper	murmur	mumble

Name: _____

Handout 28B:
Revise for Topic-Specific Words

Directions: Read through the paragraph. Cross out the underlined words and replace them with topic-specific vocabulary. Reread the paragraph to make sure it works. If there is time remaining, look for other generic words that could be replaced with topic-specific words.

Aliki and Steven Kellogg tell the <u>story</u> of Johnny Appleseed. Both books show how John Chapman <u>moved</u> west to plant a <u>bunch of apple trees</u>. But the versions have many differences. Aliki says Appleseed <u>moved</u> west after <u>people</u> were settled. Kellogg says he went to the <u>new places</u> before the pioneers. Also, Aliki says the Indians helped Appleseed when he was sick. In the Kellogg version, <u>people</u> helped him get well. Authors tell different versions of Johnny Appleseed's story.

Name: _____

Handout 29A: Prefix *un–*

Directions:

1. Box the words' prefix.
2. Determine the meaning of the words by using their prefix.
3. Figure out which word fits in each of the sentences below.

Example:

|un|tamed = ____ + _____ = not tamed (wild)

Part 1

unselfish = ____ + _____ = _____.

unafraid = ____ + _____ = _____.

unsettled = ____ + _____ = _____.

unhealthy = ____ + _____ = _____.

unbelievable = ____ + _____ = _____.

Part 2

Use the words from Part 1 in the following sentences:

1. The prairie grasses became _____ when they had no more water.

2. Pioneers thought that the land was _____ , so they moved west.

3. One-Who-Dearly-Loved-Her-People was _____ for thrusting her doll into the fire.

4. Tall Tales can be _____ .

5. John Henry was _____ of dangerous things, like working on a riverboat.

Name:

Handout 30A: Focusing Question Task 6 Evidence Organizer

Directions: Use the Keats and Lester texts to find examples of text details and illustration details about major events.

Introduction: [color red] Keats and Lester both wrote about _____.		
Topic Statement: [color green] There are differences in _____.		
	Keats	**Lester**
[color yellow] **Point 1** Difference in text		

[color blue] Point 2 Difference in illustrations		

Conclusion:
[color green]

Name:

Handout 32A: Informative Writing Checklist

Directions: After completing your informative paragraph, circle 😊 Yes or 😐 Not Yet to answer each prompt. Be sure to include a writing goal.

Reading Comprehension	Self	Peer	Teacher
I compare and contrast the two John Henry texts.	Yes Not Yet	Yes Not Yet	Yes Not Yet
Structure	**Self**	**Peer**	**Teacher**
I use an introduction with at least one similarity.	Yes Not Yet	Yes Not Yet	Yes Not Yet
I include a topic statement.	Yes Not Yet	Yes Not Yet	Yes Not Yet
I include at least two points about how the texts are different.	Yes Not Yet	Yes Not Yet	Yes Not Yet
I end the paragraph with a conclusion.	Yes Not Yet	Yes Not Yet	Yes Not Yet

Development	Self	Peer	Teacher
I choose important points that support the topic statement.	☺ ☹ Yes Not Yet	☺ ☹ Yes Not Yet	☺ ☹ Yes Not Yet
I clearly explain my points using details.	☺ ☹ Yes Not Yet	☺ ☹ Yes Not Yet	☺ ☹ Yes Not Yet
I include evidence from both texts.	☺ ☹ Yes Not Yet	☺ ☹ Yes Not Yet	☺ ☹ Yes Not Yet

Style	Self	Peer	Teacher
I use topic-specific words.	☺ ☹ Yes Not Yet	☺ ☹ Yes Not Yet	☺ ☹ Yes Not Yet

Conventions	Self	Peer	Teacher
I use capital letters at the beginning of sentences and proper nouns. **ABC**	☺ ☹ Yes Not Yet	☺ ☹ Yes Not Yet	☺ ☹ Yes Not Yet
I use end punctuation. . ? !	☺ ☹ Yes Not Yet	☺ ☹ Yes Not Yet	☺ ☹ Yes Not Yet
I write complete sentences that have subjects and verbs.	☺ ☹ Yes Not Yet	☺ ☹ Yes Not Yet	☺ ☹ Yes Not Yet
Total # of ☺:			

Name:

My writing goal is _____

_____

_____

Teacher Feedback

Name: _____

Handout 33A: Evidence Organizer for End-of-Module Task Practice

Directions: Organize evidence to respond to the question: *How was the drought in* The Legend of the Bluebonnet *different from real-life droughts in the West, like the one described in* The Buffalo Are Back?

Introduction:

[color red]

The Legend of the Bluebonnet and *The Buffalo Are Back* both describe …

Topic Statement:

[color green]

There are differences in _____.

	The Buffalo Are Back	*The Legend of the Bluebonnet*
[color yellow] Point 1		
[color blue] Point 2		

Name:

Handout 34A:
End-of-Module Evidence Organizer

Directions: Organize evidence to respond to the question: How was one legendary person (John Henry or Johnny Appleseed) different from real-life pioneers?

Introduction (Similarities)	
Topic Statement	
John Henry or **Johnny Appleseed**	**Real-life Pioneers**

Name: _____

Handout 35A:
Informative Writing Checklist

Directions: After completing your informative paragraph, circle ☺ Yes or 😐 Not Yet to answer each prompt. Be sure to include a writing goal.

Reading Comprehension	Self	Peer	Teacher
I compare and contrast John Henry or Johnny Appleseed with real-life pioneers.	Yes Not Yet	Yes Not Yet	Yes Not Yet
Structure	**Self**	**Peer**	**Teacher**
I use an introduction with at least one similarity.	Yes Not Yet	Yes Not Yet	Yes Not Yet
I include a topic statement.	Yes Not Yet	Yes Not Yet	Yes Not Yet
I include at least two points about how the texts are different.	Yes Not Yet	Yes Not Yet	Yes Not Yet
I end the paragraph with a conclusion.	Yes Not Yet	Yes Not Yet	Yes Not Yet

Development	Self	Peer	Teacher
I choose important points that support the topic statement.	☺ ☺ Yes Not Yet	☺ ☺ Yes Not Yet	☺ ☺ Yes Not Yet
I clearly explain my points using details.	☺ ☺ Yes Not Yet	☺ ☺ Yes Not Yet	☺ ☺ Yes Not Yet
I include evidence from both texts.	☺ ☺ Yes Not Yet	☺ ☺ Yes Not Yet	☺ ☺ Yes Not Yet
Style	**Self**	**Peer**	**Teacher**
I use topic-specific words.	☺ ☺ Yes Not Yet	☺ ☺ Yes Not Yet	☺ ☺ Yes Not Yet
I use adjectives in my writing.	☺ ☺ Yes Not Yet	☺ ☺ Yes Not Yet	☺ ☺ Yes Not Yet
Conventions	**Self**	**Peer**	**Teacher**
I use capital letters at the beginning of sentences and proper nouns. **ABC**	☺ ☺ Yes Not Yet	☺ ☺ Yes Not Yet	☺ ☺ Yes Not Yet
I use end punctuation. **. ? !**	☺ ☺ Yes Not Yet	☺ ☺ Yes Not Yet	☺ ☺ Yes Not Yet
I write complete sentences that have subjects and verbs.	☺ ☺ Yes Not Yet	☺ ☺ Yes Not Yet	☺ ☺ Yes Not Yet

Name: _____

I write irregular past tense verbs correctly.	☺ ☹ Yes Not Yet	☺ ☹ Yes Not Yet	☺ ☹ Yes Not Yet
I revise my paragraph's points and topic-specific words.	☺ ☹ Yes Not Yet	☺ ☹ Yes Not Yet	☺ ☹ Yes Not Yet
Total # of ☺ :			

My writing goal is _____

_____

_____

Teacher Feedback

G2 > M2 > WIT & WISDOM®

Volume of Reading Reflection Questions

Student Name: _____

Text: _____

Author: _____

Topic: _____

Genre/type of book:

Share your knowledge about Native Americans and the American West by responding to or sharing one question in each category below.

Informational

1. **Wonder:** After looking at the cover of this book, what do you notice? What do you wonder?

2. **Organize:** What topics did this book cover about the American West? What details made it interesting?

3. **Reveal:** How does the author use descriptive language or illustrations to teach you about important ideas about the West? Choose a sentence or illustration in the book that shows this important idea.

4. **Distill:** What big idea did the author want you to take away from reading this book? Find the page or line that most strongly communicates that big idea.

5. **Vocabulary:** Create a list with five items talked about in this book that you would need if you lived in the West long ago. After each word, explain the purpose of that item.

Literary

6. **Wonder:** What details do you notice about the cover that give you clues to what this story will be about?

7. **Organize:** What's happening in the text? Retell the story to a friend. Be sure to include the setting, character, problem, and resolution in your retelling. Draw the problem and how it was resolved.

8. **Reveal:** How do the illustrations in the story help you understand what life in the West was like for the characters in the story? Choose one illustration as an example.

9. **Distill:** How did the main character change from the beginning to the end of the book? Draw a picture to show how the character was at the beginning of the story and another picture to show how the character was at the end of the story.

10. **Know:** How does this story add to what you have learned about life in the West from other stories or books? Have you learned more about the West from stories or informational texts? Why?

11. **Vocabulary:** Choose three words from the story that describe the character. One word should describe how the character feels, one word the should describe what that character does, and the third word should describe what that character looks like.

WIT & WISDOM FAMILY TIP SHEET

WHAT IS MY SECOND GRADE STUDENT LEARNING IN MODULE 2?

Wit & Wisdom is our English curriculum. It builds knowledge of key topics in history, science, and literature through the study of excellent texts. By reading and responding to stories and nonfiction texts, we will build knowledge of the following topics:

Module 1: A Season of Change

Module 2: The American West

Module 3: Civil Rights Heroes

Module 4: Good Eating

In this second module, *The American West*, we will study the growth that came from the struggle of early settlers and pioneers. By analyzing texts and art, students answer the question, What was life like in the West for early Americans?

OUR CLASS WILL READ THESE BOOKS:

Picture Books (Informational)

- *Journey of a Pioneer*, Patricia J. Murphy
- *Plains Indians*, Andrew Santella
- *The Buffalo Are Back*, Jean Craighead George

Picture Books (Literary)

- *John Henry*, Julius Lester
- *John Henry: An American Legend*, Ezra Jack Keats
- *Johnny Appleseed*, Steven Kellogg
- *The Legend of the Bluebonnet*, Tomie dePaola
- *The Story of Johnny Appleseed*, Aliki

Poetry

- "Buffalo Dusk," Carl Sandburg

OUR CLASS WILL EXAMINE THIS PAINTING:

- *Among the Sierra Nevada, California*, Albert Bierstadt

OUR CLASS WILL ASK THESE QUESTIONS:

- How did the actions of American Indians and early Americans impact the prairie in the American West?
- What was life like for Plains Indians in the early American West?
- What was life like for pioneers in the early American West?
- What life lesson can we learn from the story of Bluebonnet?
- How do different authors tell the story of Johnny Appleseed's life?
- What life lesson can we learn from the story of John Henry?

QUESTIONS TO ASK AT HOME:

As you read with your second grade student, ask:

- What's happening?
- What does a closer look at words and illustrations reveal about this text's deeper meaning?

BOOKS TO READ AT HOME:

- *New York's Bravest*, Mary Pope Osborne
- *Cowboys and Cowgirls: Yippee-Yay!*, Gail Gibbons
- *Locomotive*, Brian Floca
- *The Legend of the Indian Paintbrush*, Tomie dePaola
- *The Rough-Face Girl*, Rafe Martin
- *Bill Pickett: Rodeo-Ridin' Cowboy*, Andrea Davis Pinkney

IDEAS FOR TALKING ABOUT THE AMERICAN WEST:

Visit the library together. Ask the librarian to recommend a book on the American West, or select one of the titles in the list above. Take a look at the illustrations with your second grade student and ask:

- What do you notice and wonder about this illustration?
- Who were the early Americans?
- How did they live their lives?
- How did they deal with the challenges of a developing nation?
- What was life like in the American West?

CREDITS

Great Minds® has made every effort to obtain permission for the reprinting of all copyrighted material. If any owner of copyrighted material is not acknowledged herein, please contact Great Minds® for proper acknowledgment in all future editions and reprints of this module.

- All material from the *Common Core State Standards for English Language Arts & Literacy in History/Social Studies, Science, and Technical Subjects* © Copyright 2010 National Governors Association Center for Best Practices and Council of Chief State School Officers. All rights reserved.
- All images are used under license from Shutterstock.com unless otherwise noted.
- For updated credit information, please visit **http://witeng.link/credits**.

ACKNOWLEDGMENTS

Great Minds® Staff

The following writers, editors, reviewers, and support staff contributed to the development of this curriculum.

Karen Aleo, Elizabeth Bailey, Ashley Bessicks, Sarah Brenner, Ann Brigham, Catherine Cafferty, Sheila Byrd-Carmichael, Lauren Chapalee, Emily Climer, Rebecca Cohen, Elaine Collins, Julia Dantchev, Beverly Davis, Shana Dinner de Vaca, Kristy Ellis, Moira Clarkin Evans, Marty Gephart, Mamie Goodson, Nora Graham, Lindsay Griffith, Lorraine Griffith, Christina Gonzalez, Emily Gula, Brenna Haffner, Joanna Hawkins, Elizabeth Haydel, Sarah Henchey, Trish Huerster, Ashley Hymel, Carol Jago, Mica Jochim, Jennifer Johnson, Mason Judy, Sara Judy, Lior Klirs, Shelly Knupp, Liana Krissoff, Sarah Kushner, Suzanne Lauchaire, Diana Leddy, David Liben, Farren Liben, Brittany Lowe, Whitney Lyle, Stephanie Kane-Mainier, Liz Manolis, Jennifer Marin, Audrey Mastroleo, Maya Marquez, Susannah Maynard, Cathy McGath, Emily McKean, Andrea Minich, Rebecca Moore, Lynne Munson, Carol Paiva, Michelle Palmieri, Tricia Parker, Marya Myers Parr, Meredith Phillips, Eden Plantz, Shilpa Raman, Rachel Rooney, Jennifer Ruppel, Julie Sawyer-Wood, Nicole Shivers, Danielle Shylit, Rachel Stack, Amelia Swabb, Vicki Taylor, Melissa Thomson, Lindsay Tomlinson, Tsianina Tovar, Sarah Turnage, Melissa Vail, Keenan Walsh, Michelle Warner, Julia Wasson, Katie Waters, Sarah Webb, Lynn Welch, Yvonne Guerrero Welch, Amy Wierzbicki, Margaret Wilson, Sarah Woodard, Lynn Woods, and Rachel Zindler

Colleagues and Contributors

We are grateful for the many educators, writers, and subject-matter experts who made this program possible.

David Abel, Robin Agurkis, Sarah Ambrose, Rebeca Barroso, Julianne Barto, Amy Benjamin, Andrew Biemiller, Charlotte Boucher, Adam Cardais, Eric Carey, Jessica Carloni, Dawn Cavalieri, Janine Cody, Tequila Cornelious, David Cummings, Matt Davis, Thomas Easterling, Jeanette Edelstein, Sandra Engleman, Charles Fischer, Kath Gibbs, Natalie Goldstein, Laurie Gonsoulin, Dennis Hamel, Kristen Hayes, Steve Hettleman, Cara Hoppe, Libby Howard, Gail Kearns, Lisa King, Sarah Kopec, Andrew Krepp, Shannon Last, Ted MacInnis, Christina Martire, Alisha McCarthy, Cindy Medici, Brian Methe, Ivonne Mercado, Patricia Mickelberry, Jane Miller, Cathy Newton, Turi Nilsson, Julie Norris, Tara O'Hare, Galemarie Ola, Tamara Otto, Christine Palmtag, Dave Powers, Jeff Robinson, Karen Rollhauser, Tonya Romayne, Emmet Rosenfeld, Mike Russoniello, Deborah Samley, Casey Schultz, Renee Simpson, Rebecca Sklepovich, Kim Taylor, Tracy Vigliotti, Charmaine Whitman, Glenda Wisenburn-Burke, and Howard Yaffe

Early Adopters

The following early adopters provided invaluable insight and guidance for Wit & Wisdom:

- Bourbonnais School District 53 • Bourbonnais, IL
- Coney Island Prep Middle School • Brooklyn, NY
- Gate City Charter School for the Arts • Merrimack, NH
- Hebrew Academy for Special Children • Brooklyn, NY
- Paris Independent Schools • Paris, KY
- Saydel Community School District • Saydel, IA
- Strive Collegiate Academy • Nashville, TN
- Valiente College Preparatory Charter School • South Gate, CA
- Voyageur Academy • Detroit, MI

Design Direction provided by Alton Creative, Inc.

Project management support, production design and copyediting services provided by ScribeConcepts.com

Copyediting services provided by Fine Lines Editing

Product management support provided by Sandhill Consulting